BECOMING JUDAS

BECOMING JUDAS

poems

Nicelle Davis

illustrations

Cheryl Gross

Red Hen Press | *Pasadena, CA*

Book design and layout by Skyler Schulze

Library of Congress Cataloging-in-Publication Data

Davis, Nicelle, 1979–

[Poems. Selections]

Becoming Judas : poems / Nicelle Davis; illustrations, Cheryl Gross.—First edition.

  pages cm

ISBN 978-1-59709-239-5 (alk. paper)

I. Title.

PS3604.A97268B43 2013

811'.6—dc23

2013008907

The National Endowment for the Arts, the Los Angeles County Arts Commission, the Los Angeles Department of Cultural Affairs, the City of Pasadena Cultural Affairs Division, Sony Pictures Entertainment, and the Dwight Stuart Youth Fund partially support Red Hen Press.

First Edition

Published by Red Hen Press

www.redhen.org

ACKNOWLEDGMENTS

Earlier versions of these poems appeared in the following journals:

31ˢᵗ *Bird, Bad Light, Breadcrumb Scabs, Caesura, Connotation Press, Elimae, Escape Into Life, FuseLit, The Houston Literary Review, Illya's Honey, The Mom Egg, Moulin Review, Mudlicious, The New York Quarterly, Offending Adam, PANK, Pedestal, Redactions: Poetry & Poetics, Superficial Flesh, Tin Foil Dress, Transcurrent Literary Journal, Two Review, Verdad,* and *Weave.*

Great thanks to Dennis Mecham for his gifts as a photographer and Pavlina Janssen for her creative works as a costumer. The cover image is a creation of their combined talents.

for my mother
—Nicelle Davis

With all my love, Louis and Harley
—Cheryl Gross

Contents

LIST OF ILLUSTRATIONS

BECOMING JUDAS

Genesis:
Origins of a Homemade Religion

The Missing Text in the Gospel of Judas

Salvation:

[a door opening onto another

[[full rotation; self-begotten, I am, threshold.
Devouring light to be light. Every child is
a knob turning inward. Language of swallow-
ing. Forever.]]

joyful / joyful]

Alternative Salvation I:

[here, take your missing—

[[fornication—that loud dress of stitched together
crows. You at the center of how hard wings
beat when feet are tethered. Lick your hand,
taste how he would have. In the wild orange
poppies, your (un) conceived daughter reads
a script sprawled across the blue wall above
her. She translates the word. All understood.
All is mutually felt.]]

it is. / it is.]

Alternative Salvation II:

[there is your lost

[[propped in a chair. Her face covered in dust.
She's been waiting for the spider to finish
spinning her silver jacket. She's renounced
opening her eyes. Now is your chance.
The weaver stops its movements. You feel
that spool of yarn in your throat unraveling.
I love you]]

mother hears you / mother believes you]

CONTEMPORARY PROPHETS

A crow plucks a sparrow from the sky like fruit
from a vine. The palm-bird, visible
from the thick-billed Corvus, gags the devouring
mouth. Rhythms quick for life—
this street a swollen larynx. Lamentations. In flight,
the crow—size of a human torso—
chokes. Wings pulled inward. The sparrow is let go—
a crow left to hunger.

Disclaimer: Assumptions Made by This Homemade Religion

Interval: [in-ter-vuhl] the relationship between the pitch of two notes.

> My myths crossed when I was four. I mistook the pastel picture
> of Jesus hung in every Mormon home for John Lennon. Both
> called the Prince of Peace. Was encouraged to talk to him. Offer
> up suffering. Let him carry my scabs in his satchel; red letters
> addressed home. Inside the paper-wrapped package: a six-string
> guitar interpreting lyrics. I still talk to John when praying to Jesus.

Pitch: [pich] frequency of a sound.

> Driving four hours a day.   John plays with wind out the window.
> I chase kites slipped out from the grasp of children. Sky Diamonds:
> Red, Yellow, Blue.   [love]   *John / Jesus why'd you leave Cynthia?*
> Blue. Red. Yellow. [hope]   **Why are you talking to a dead man?**
> Yellow. Blue. Red.   [life]   *Damn it. I missed my favorite color.*
> **Well, fuckin' leave me/me alone and pay attention to your own.**

Frequency: [free-kwuhn-see] number of occurrences repeating per unit time.

> The men who killed John / Jesus were after light. Afraid the dark
> would swallow them.   The flesh wounds are real.   Holes in Jesus
> the size of hands.   **We like to think of them as body pockets,**
> John tells me. They say,   **Go ahead,   reach in   and pull out**
> **a strawberry.**   *Hell no,* I say.
> **We know you   are hungry,**
> they say. *Could   n't we just be*
> *friends?* I urge   **Out of your**
> **league,** they hiss. *I'd rather starve,* I spit. **Desire is a snake in your**
> **pancake batter. It will eat you whole while you**
> **long for home-cooked bread.**

Octave: [ok-tiv, -teyv] relationship; a natural phenomenon referred to as the basic miracle of music. The human ear tends to hear both notes as essentially the same.

[We are music

baking in the body's hot center]

The Unsaid Prayer Found in the God-Size Hole

Tie legs of old pantyhose to a bent clothes-
hanger. Catch my heart. Cage it in plastic
strawberry carts. Feed it cabbage and keep
it from flying   recklessly   towards fire.

Issues with Ego in Song and Prayer

The Gospel of Judas   Jesus says, *it's possible for you*
brought up   *to reach the mysteries of the Kingdom*
from a crypt—   *but you will grieve—*

same year as: polyester is in fashion

cult leader Charles   Manson sings, *Old ego is*
releases the album *Lies*   *a too much thing*
to finance his defense   *He'll make you fool yourself*

and the Beatles   McCartney says, *the thing*
dissolves.   *is over.*

God, come down. Right now. Before someone gets hurt.

HARMONY:

separate vibrations fall into gaps of another vibration to create wholeness.

> John Lennon speaks like a whip
> in the T.V. temple of lights, fire
> roars at a church album burning,
> a radio plays, *Please, Please Me.*

A balance—

> as fire hops the fence to devour mountains,
> Jesus sings from a rock-star-suicidal;
> all of one source will return to that source.

—between tension and resolve. Lord, *please, please* forgive me

> for(ever) doubting.

Chapter One
Where'd that Angel Fly Off To?

The Golden Plates went missing. This should be easy enough to understand—the most sought things are often slippery—needless to say, if God made them, the polish would be perfect—slick as sliced Spam in your hands.

2 Cut Joseph a break, he'd just seen angels, and from what I've heard, celestials work in symbols and archetypal images. In other words, they are what can be remembered.

Chapter Two
Angels as Plague or Pleasure. You Choose.

Joseph lost them, just as the stone tablets were mis-shuffled in a pile of Judaic To-Do lists—most likely shredded by lightning to prevent identity theft.

2 Interesting to me is how angels are constantly dividing and re-dividing themselves like cells—the rebellious ones, as cancer, refusing to die.

3 And just like cartoons, they are many and more—the best getting their own amusement parks with mascot imitations for photo-ops.

Chapter Three
The Closest I've come to Being an Angel

Wanting to understand furries I rented a chicken costume to have sex with my husband. I was perched on the sink flapping mad. He penetrated twice before loosing his hard-on, the whole thing as damaging as imagining sex with his mother.

2 I always wondered how my parents conceived me, my mother hating to be touched. I was in awe of children who "accidentally" walked in on their moms spread-eagle—saw firsthand the bushfire once worn as a crown.

Chapter Four
Renaming Angels

Prophet Smith's favorite seraph, the macaroni-colored one, known as "The Burning One," he renamed Moroni—archangel in charge of unleashing the universal conflagration.

2 Joseph had an odd sense of fun—playing checkers with his wives by candlelight, all confused as to whose turn it was to go against him.

Chapter Five
I Choose.

If angels were sold as furry plush toys—hands down—I'd pick Azrael: he who causes the realm of thought to fall into the world of paper, like the making of a religion—all possible. Let's say *feathers and checkers* are acts of salvation. Forever and Ever. Amen.

CHRONICLES:
ORDER OF GENETICS

1970–

My mom moves to Fort Walton Beach from Okinawa,
where *mamazons* made dresses

for her dollies and cut down yard snakes for soup. She
brags about eating cocao-

covered ants. This is the summer a man will break into
her room and (*almost*) rape

her. She ignores the war (*mostly*). She likes to string jewelry.
Her father's an officer in the Air

Force; her mom finds birth control in a drawer. The pills
are her sister's, but she will be

called the whore. I hate my mother (*most*) for not naming
blame. If not for her I'd never

be a poet. She's who put me in this blue dress lit on fire—
taught me to speak, not of burning,

but how pretty the dress. 1970s when I'd most liked to
have known her. She says, *Florida is*

where I was most happy. I say, *watch Ma, as I twirl the flame's lift.*

As I Fall Asleep Reading Revelations in My Grandmother's House

Ms. Fire-tongue pours tea; Earl Gray turns to spiders as its warmth hits her mouth; their dark bodies scatter across her face, rest in her hair.

2   The legs on the pink velvet chair are longer than mine; I ask for a walk by the river; she sucks lemons; I take her hand; spiders make a rush for the bridge of our linked arms.

3   At first, the light at the door is blinding; our eyes adjust with each step on a road turning to water; cobwebs grow from the crown of our heads, streaming.

4   I sing as though a ship is caught in my swallow; she holds her lips tight against sorrows rising; I thought my joy was hers; I was wrong.

5   In the river she turns into a teething-pike gumming my left arm; I never meant to fear her, but the water is thick with sensation—current and scales.

6   I grab onto sunlight and swing us to shore; she can't breath; I put my mouth over her gills; she finds breath in saliva.

7   She grows human; she grows young; we clap our hands and sing: *Down-by-the-banks of the hanky-panky*; stars jump out from clouds; surprised, we laugh.

8   In the moss we tell stories by half-sleep. We make plans. Tomorrow we'll go fishing in Lake Lit on Fire.

My Mother's First Orphaned Christmas

The bodies are dressed in green.
People comment on what a good
job the parlor has done painting
their faces to look lively. The line
is long. Bride and groom next to
each other, waiting for their long-
car exit. Their eldest daughter,
       your sister,
bends to their stiff lips, cries—
a cup drops,
       the ceramic breaks
into halves. She thrusts herself
into the coffin, then
       her husband
collects her
       to composure.

There are a few acts
still left within our control.

Carbon Monoxide Poisoning

> What is pronounced strengthens.
>> —Czesław Miłosz

blue flame. faulty furnace. combustion.

———————————

Before she found her parents'
bodies stacked like lovers,
asphyxiated—

before she chalked herself not
with lime, but with speed
and nights spent

organizing the kitchen, labeling
spoons: SPOONS, forks: FORKS—
until all things had a name,

an absolute reason for being—
J. R. was my mother.

———————————

My Grandmother's Last Words: *Lately I've been seeing ghosts. Never thought I'd be a believer. Even bought a Ouiji Board. Always the answer is yes. Constantly the sound of footsteps. I want to know where the dead are going. Always the answer is yes. How much easier death is, knowing there'll be company. Even now God is in my kitchen licking a wooden spoon clean.*

———————————

I hold a fork and spoon up
to my son who
is cautiously approaching
language. I say
spoon, fork. He understands
these are the answers
without knowing the birds
I'm pronouncing.

———————————

Spoon: a cupped hand extended in offering. Fork: fingers grasping substance.

Enough Time

There is a cold river being pulled through the eye of a needle—hands scarred
by fire from putting a baby out—white nightgown up with a match—these

fingers pinch and pull a silver thread down my back. She is my grandmother.
I am seven. She is making me a black velvet dress for Christmas, but hasn't

time for a zipper. She is married to a man who at twelve tosses his five siblings
from a second story window before dragging his father's kerosene doused body

from their burning house. Flesh separating from bone—a paper man. A rasp-
breath effort: that final unsaid word. His father will melt in his arms. Stick to

his skin. He will drop bombs in Vietnam. She will sell vacuums door to door
with two girls, twins, a baby trailing behind her. Her children: curious matches.

My mother will have red moons burned into her belly with a cigarette lighter.
Her sister, at fifty, won't know why. They will leave their mother in a dentist's

waiting room. They will be hours late in picking her up. A cup of blood in her
mouth. She will say nothing when they fetch her. Her husband will use her false

teeth as a puppet. Chase after his wife with her own bite. I want to love her gums,
but she refuses to undress her mouth in front of me. At Christmas dinner, when

the conversations is years away from me—I arch my back to break the dress seam—
for the sound of tearing open—for the attention of coming apart. I think it will be

funny. This is the only time I will see my grandmother cry. Later she will tell
me stories of the Great Depression—how she spent money to see a flushing toilet.

She will have me piss in a pot to understand. She will promise to bare smile when I turn sixteen. She will look at her hands and say, *we do what we can—even when it isn't*

enough. You understand? I will nod yes and mean no. She will die when I am thirteen. I'll never feel like I loved her enough. I'll love her more than any.

The star that leads the way is your
star, Judas,
for you will sacrifice the human body
that swallows me.

Bless us with the stop of us, Judas. Dress your neck with a tress of blue tongues and dust. Someone must deliver that animated dead thing of a kiss. There must be a giver of that silver strand of singing spittle upon my face. Now sew your own words closed. Dig the earth out from under you. Moan as your soul is ripped like birth from your belly. Burst upon the field of blood with the pain of how you loved beyond how love could love you. You, be the state of constant want, so all the rest can have me.

Jesus fed him yeast and vines
to make the 13th god rise up from
Judas's head towards the shine
of copper coins. *Sacrifice*
needs suicide needs
betrayal to be soft
as a slow kiss
in a garden.

Theory-Based Explanation for Sound

a thrust into dissipation—

Proverbs:
Middle School and Other Maladies

Jesus and Judas as Boys

Judas, bury me in the sand.
       I don't wanna.
Come on. I'll let you use my glass shovel.
       Leave me alone already.
Don't make me make a miracle of you.
       I'm busy.
Put that dolly away and start digging.
       It's a Roman Guard with special Whip-Motion-Action.
Dolly.
       It's *not* a dolly.

       You broke Pontius.
I didn't touch him.
       You didn't have to. You broke it.
Prove it.
       I hate you.
You don't know the half of hating. Now. Start digging.

When I Was a Boy

My mother bent a Lamborghini on a hydrant, crossing the street in a pair of stilettos. Men couldn't stop looking.

She knew the values of being wanted. My bowed nose concerned her. She always asking if I'd been touched. Yet.

Where I shouldn't. I cut off all my hair—lived on the highest limb of a tree. As a tomboy, I gave her less to worry

about. Out-wrestled the sixth-grade. Taught myself, *no. Ding-dong*, a Sarah Jane Adams Elementary boy said, pushing my ten-

year-old nipple. Opening a door. *You'll appreciate being wanted one day*, mother said, rubbing the bump out of the rim of my nose.

What I wanted was her—the way I wished for a branch to grow past where I climbed— to be lifted without others spading for our roots.

The Mother of Invention

1820, Joseph Smith is 14 years old
                    at the Second Great Awakening.
                                      The thick ropes of evangelical
voices are drawn tight over heaven
                                  to tether God to the ground.
Too many tongues on fire, to hear
                    a pre-teen in the kitchen saying,   *Dear*
                              Father, make me
a tuna fish sandwich.   He faints
                    hits his head on the table.   Wakes saying,
I saw an angel.   *He had wings*   *like a shark's mouth*
            and spoke   *like Shakespeare.*
Now,   *will someone please*   *pour me*   *a glass of milk?*

When in Doubt, Ask Yourself,
What Would Jesus Do?

Jesus said, *Damn the soul that depends on the flesh.*

––––––––––––

At thirteen
it was en vogue
to strangle each
other until *slip*—
       our bodies lay
       limp as clothes
       on the floor. Self
       striped to an act
of singing—
sine curve in
oscillation.
In blackout
       a field of light
       rolls like an ocean
       of fire, euphoria,
       before
the automatic
pull back to
consciousness—
another world.

––––––––––––

Jesus said, *Damn the flesh that depends on the soul.*

––––––––––––

I've never shot a gun.
The man who meant to teach me
the etiquette of it
took his head off with a .44 before
we made it to the range.

————————————

Jesus and Jesus
are wrangling
over spare change.

Today this / Tomorrow that.

Stolen from the Mouth of Thunder

Sonic Boom:
impulsive noise. Caused by an object
moving faster than sound. Released
from an unseen mouth is a sky dirge wailing . . .

———————————

Zee's open-bellied toad
of a car was all intestines
and heart—lubricated pistons
pumping her across
the southwest, trying to outrun
the genetics of her mother's
schizophrenia. Zee's hood,
ripped off by the wind,
was abandoned somewhere
between Utah and Arizona.

We'd drive across town
to Liberty Park, where black
rubber swings held us as
we drank Captain Morgan
mixed with 7-Eleven Slurpies,
smoking American
Spirits. We'd thrust
ourselves towards
the dark curve of the sky
singing,

I'd watch the gaps
between Zee's teeth
stacked like faces of a choir
begging God to hear her.

———————————

. . . I am a mute who does not speak,
and great is my multitude of words.
I am the silence that is incomprehensible
and the idea whose remembrance is frequent.
I am the voice whose sound is manifold
and the word whose appearance is multiple.

And He Believe(d):
A Brief History of Joseph Smith

When he closes his eyes, the light through
branches transforms into shapes of effortless
swimming. Above him. Diving. Rising. Ebb
taking the parameters of a shore. Flow filling
the corners of caverns—a smooth wash over
all complication. Simply was. Simply is. Why
not this be God? Why not? God was / God is.

As Songs Can Travel Past Their Singers

When she knew you were in her,
                she clawed off her skin and lay
                                sensation like a pair of nylon
                                                stockings over a space heater.
                        With the smell of toasting legs,
                she lathered her raw body in sea
salt and oil. Lavender jam; scent
                like the summer she planted seeds
                                in an egg carton to grow a bouquet
                                                for her father's grave. She was five
                        when the bed of a semi-truck took
                his body off. He sold life insurance.
Her mother bought her gold high-
                tops and beat her. Last I knew,
                                she was rewinding the image of her
                                                lover fucking another woman on
                        a camcorder. I told her to stop
                watching but she couldn't stop.
Daily doses of acid put a skip in her
                record. That is to say, she'd just come
                                out of the shower—convulsing naked
                under me as I tried to contain her fit.
The only other time I held her naked
                was the day she was born. We were
                                almost sisters. We were kids with purple
                popsicle beards. We played M.A.S.H.
We circled the number: you. We waited.
                In a cold tube, her Father appeared
                                as a gathering of wings singing, *I have*
                                                yellow feathers to weave into a dress

for you. She sent him scattering in
a fractured migration. Let's just say,
she had the knife that could have
picked the lock on heaven, but
she wouldn't go where she couldn't
take you. She birthed and left you.
Without you, she sings for you;
a song traveling the distance
in a lineage of broken birds.

Psalms and Lamentations:
All You Need Is Love

APPLE

Inside story—"The Beatles' Break-up"—runs every year at Christmas,
  the key players see more with every recollection. Re-mastered.
  Re-released.

Jesus, suckles / John nurses. bottles. needles. To say J. didn't have
  a carnal understanding of women would be incomplete. J.
  collects tears in the grail

of his mouth. No time for hot wax. J. devours his lovers. God took,
  from Mary, flesh to cloak his son but this is not the same as
  having a mother source. Motherless sons.

It's a type. Born in a manger, the dearth doesn't wash off easily. You
  can see him all over her. *We gave up everything*, Yoko says, and
  by everything she means daughters. Once the fellow-

ship ends, John tells Yoko, *you be everything for me now, "ok?"* Jesus
  has Mary wash his feet with the loose strands of her hair—
  texture of slippage between his toes. A mattress is

installed in the studio. A tension builds. The King sweats blood
  in a garden. When searching for reasons for the break,
  it's easy to point at the dragon. But there were men, too—

who slept while the devil-plant sprouted fruit. John told reporters,
  if the label Apple losses any more money, the Beatles will
  bankrupt soon. Peter, didn't take kindly to his shortcomings

being spread in text. McCartney, if given the chance, would have
        bitten off Mary's fingers to prevent her from touching his
        Jesus. He realized she emboldened J. *She pushed him, he*

liked that, McCartney says. She had him. *Do it more. Do it double.*
        Take all your clothes off. Be nailed down and suspended.
        She says, *Behold your son* dangling from my nipple.

Jesus Propositions Judas

We ought to cut
each other from our skin-tethers—
quit this arithmetic
      of oxygen,
            rubidium,
                  and flash of blue.

We could have just as easily been violet fireworks,
but are not,
not even with the potential of spontaneous combustion.

The star compounds in us
      are explosives disarmed
            by the wet of our bodies.

Hot July, Jesus says, *Stop struggling against me and give us a kiss.*

The Rape of Aeons

Two angels arrive at Sodom—
their skin made of dawn
and dusk—emanate a stream
of touch. Whoever they pass
feels the weight of all they ever
loved upon them. The guiltless
approach of all loves—to have
at once—

A man feels the warmth of his
mother's lap while the hand
of the round-eyed girl leads
a trail of scratch-marks down
his back. He collapses. Cries.
The cat he drowned in a river
curves its soft body,
like comfort, around his feet.

A woman feels tear-shaped
bodies of rats scurry out
from the tunnel of her mouth.
Rodents scream as she has
wanted to, *do not leave me*.
The hands of her husband layer
seven years of caress through
her hair. She weaves her face
between these fingers of light.

With the dead made alive—
forgiveness found in the textures
of return—how could they not
go to Lot's house, demanding
that the angels be brought for
them to have intercourse with
the past, present, and future—
to conceive an understanding
of what all this suffering is for.

All the Hope Found in the Scent of Sickness

Overnight our bodies have held to
the overlap of one heat upon another.
Between us is a seeping, a balm pouring
from cankers. The resin, sweat as myrrh
carefully dug from the wounds of trees.

Priests burn such scabs in censers,
rocking smoke from golden chains.
Soot gasping onto walls, dust longing
to be with dust. There will always be
a part of us that refuses to dissipate.

Stains of us sully the whole house.
I leave lipstick on the rim of a cup.
You collect pennies in a large jar.
We talk about, one day, visiting
the *Commiphora* fields. We will

watch them struggle up from under
the weight of one blessing upon another.
Their flowers sparking from branches
grown for pyres to devour the past whole.

By the Bible's Map, We Have Lost the Location of Love

Your hands trace the bars of my cage—
the two halves of ribs suggesting that I
hinge open where your fingers travel
in the direction of a changed lexicon—
stopping at my sternum. Our Biblical
use of the word kidney has moved from
behind floating arches to the bone-cased
heart. What read as *pissing* now *pumps*.
Love no longer has the satisfaction of
emptying—but is a cold fire circulating.

Flash: Leibovitz's Photo of John and Yoko

Polaroid: Yoko Ono, in jeans and a black sweater lies on her back, a straight line. Her hair surges, above her head, a rooted chaos. She's a rib sucked dry of flesh. He kisses her cheek. She's unaffected. His touch adds only another layer to her. He looks like he knows the bullet's coming. Five times coming.

He's lost her once already. She's still cold from being in ear-shot of the sound of him with another woman. Together they have survived each other. John curls naked and fetus-style at her side. His arms frame her face. His legs, bent into inverted V's, encase her torso. Captured: the sight of a man becoming a shrine.

Asleep with Jesus

The ground is a full church without singing.

THE SONGS OF SONGS:
IMAGINE

Imagine

I.

Wind pours in and out of you like sand.
I turn like a dust devil. You jump. I pull
the rug out from under the sky. I unravel
earth strands. They go to pieces of will-
ow trees. Branches everywhere. Swing.
All is falling. Without end. Call it love.

II.

Skin kites. Red mud water turned to blood.
Gone, all gone. Instead, a field of over
grown grass. Green fading to gold. There
she is. You see her. And your son. Appear.
Disappear. Land dolphins in oceans of grain.
They are safe. They are happy. They are.

III.

. . . but I'm not the only one

IV.

I lighten my grip. You lighten your teeth. Our
bodies go lax. Slip right off the bone. We make
love without bodies. Nothing in the way. I ask
you to stay. You say, there is no such thing as
stay. We laugh like kids at church. We can't stop.
The trouble we're in is the greatest joke ever told.

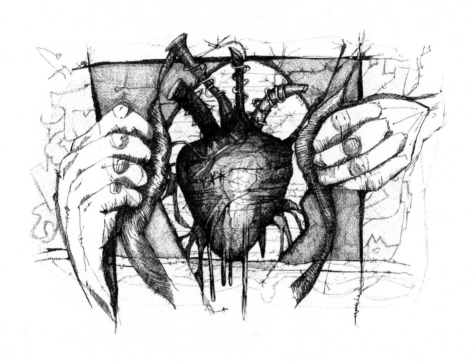

New Testament:
Beautiful Boy (Darling Boy)

Faith as Seen on YouTube

I. Contemporary Gnostics

He seems to be
kissing more than speaking
words. His fellow Gnostic spokes-
model transitions into frame—her face an orb
of light dimmed to a long-legged brunette. Mention
the Knights of Templar and his eyes flash with Hollywood
potential. Imagined rescue
—she's tied to a chair by the arms of her own cardigan—
obviously the work of Papist conspirators. She'll
say, *truth will be sought by the few*—rebels
moaning softly in University Libraries.
There is more than just this body,
she'll say. *Oh yes,* he'll
say, *more. more.*

II. Because I've Heard it Before

I'm not converted. Joseph Smith went down—
with his six shooters firing—from a window
for something similar to gnosis. He knew
it was over. Angry mob with ropes
noosed. He wanted life more
than salvation. Reached
for the blue hands
of God before
the ground
caught
him.

Something more (like gravity) is out there. A martyr is
born from the earth of Missouri; like a turnip. Belief.
Like harvest. I'm sown and born in Utah. I never asked
for this religion, never asked for gravity. A root food isn't
choosy—it will grow anywhere—with its ability to
prevent famine. His was a con, but such a necessary con.

Joe
said "I
do" to 33
women, before
the gig was up. As
he came down, a promise
for love manifested itself—as
light turned to flesh in a mild root.
I won't be a fool-bride but the pains of
starvation are a mother's hands in my soil
digging to save her children from the absence
                              of Heaven's feast.

III. Broadcast Yourself

Originally I wrote *tit* instead of *lip* when describing the sexual tension between young
missionaries. Their knowing beyond   knowing like lovers hanging from
cords of ecstasy—refusing to   come down, makes my
eyes hatch locusts from   staring too long at
their lights shining   from my laptop.

I know only chance. My

feet will / won't

hit ground.

Bet   any-
thing the night before Judas died, he paid some mouth to call him child.
Tell the ground to come for me—he asked the prostitute. *Tell the world I meant no harm.* I don't
know why love is deemed legitimate for some and not others. I tell you Judas loved Jesus
enough to die for him. The hanging body: a pornographic image. I tell you, there are
those of us who must fall; our faith an all-in wager. We jump, praying:

Let there be light.

The Woman Who Cut Judas Down

had lost her son. This body strung
from a branch could be anyone—
even hers. She climbed the tree
to chew through the rope
and bring down the stopped
heart that had grown within her.

On the ground she gathered him to her—
whole self shaking as a baptism
worked its way out from in her
words beyond human articulation—
fever and a cry mistaken for pain.

Paul McCartney / Julian Lennon 1985 CBS Interview (Recounted from Memory)

McCartney:

I never got to straighten things out—but what I have to take
is my consolation—I'll take anything I can get as a consolation.

The last phone call. We talked about cats. Yoko dialed later.
Said, you know he did love you. You grab anything you can get.

I know we came close. To love / hate. But any strong relationship
seems to have that in it. I think. Pity. Nothing is simple.

Julian Lennon:

The simplicity of the music made him great. I think of my dad
as a wise uncle. Well that's what I get from the albums. But it's
the simplicity of it—you just say it straightforward rather than
writing a book about it. I've only slowly over the years begun to
realize the whole thing with him being away.

Let Us Say, This Is the End of the World

Wire-cords snapping. After that, we all went to some kind of jail.

I was watching one boy and his imaginary gun making out in front of my apartment
while 300,000 Christmas lights lit Temple Square like the mouth of God shining on

cow piss and ice. The thrush is he was nice. No the truth is his name was cancer
like my mother's. So I drew a door on the sidewalk with chalk and flew to California

with a suitcase crammed full of clothes left on their hangers. Lived like a cat
in some guy's house until I couldn't. We did a lot of grooming and called it healing.

I wrote my first sonnet for a boy that rhyme tweekers with sneakers though now I would
do it slant like bikers or knickers. Then we got married.
And now we are parents.

WHEN FAILURE REACHES HEIGHTS OF EPIC VICTORY

The light opens against my back and travels as a fire born
without fingers. I question
birth's diversion: Doesn't the moon look lovely, resting on
that thin line of diminishing
day? Its halo outshines depth—distance of stars overtaken
by glow, transforming night
into a reachable body: a bone-colored world. Round as my
baby's face. The space
between his breath and my watch. Memory reduced to this
light opening: he will
know none of this, while I live in a web of overlapping skies.

Detours in Faith

I. She lives

with 6 cats in a 12 room house. Love box. Broken when her lover left
she transformed every room into a holding cell for near music. Filled 1
room (floor to ceiling) with cracked guitars. Piano parts up the stairwell.
Kitchen of drum heads. Cat shit throughout. She tells me when *life is
bigger than a poem, stop. God damn it girl. Stop. Before you miss . . .*

II. They've cut the rest

out. She told them to take it all after the 5th miscarriage. Couldn't take
the room of women waiting heartbeats. Not when the doctors were
checking for the stop in her—the drop from her. She tells me, *I lost God.
Cried for a week. Never wanted to loose that magic, but once it's gone . . .*

III. In Denmark

(according to my mother) there is no religion. All are happy. Have
humanity. Instead. Leave their babies in the street while they shop.
Cars swerve. I think *she must be using again. No one is watching her . . .*

IV. My friend says

she wants *to take as many with her as possible.* Be the lifeboat. I hear
her say, *I'd rather drown than leave the drowning to . . .*

V. Today I have

the impulse to throw myself to the ground and dig—not for hole—
but for scarred ground—for scratched open skin—for rocks to bruise
me back. Earth rubbed into my body—prayer. *God* (if you are there) *I hate . . .*

VI. Falling at the wheel

surrounded by glass. Reflections everywhere. I slap my face with cold
air pushed through a window. The force of entrance. 70 miles per hour.
Yellow dashes. Exits. I'm always fighting sleep. *I can't afford to miss . . .*

Commuter's Lament

I sing doo-wop while driving Highway 138
as if traveling Ecclesiastes's silver cord towards
my endless and excessive devotion to books.
A radio forecast predicts a storm approaching.

I change stations to find a rhythm. At the red
light, I draw a dark line correctly across both
eyelids. Rub the blue ring bruise where you
mistook biting for kissing. The almond trees

are blooming. You are unfolding like a blossom.
I am always returning. I lost your first steps to
the indifferent ground. I miss your face shaped
like mine. We only have a few years to spend

like shadows on the wall. I'll make you silhouettes.
A rabbit. Alligator. Pigeons circling home. I catch
the alphabet in a hand-bound book for you. None
of the symbols spell how your laughter sounds

as a thousand wings escape from the bent metal
cage of my throat.

LETTERS:
HOW DO YOU SLEEP AT NIGHT

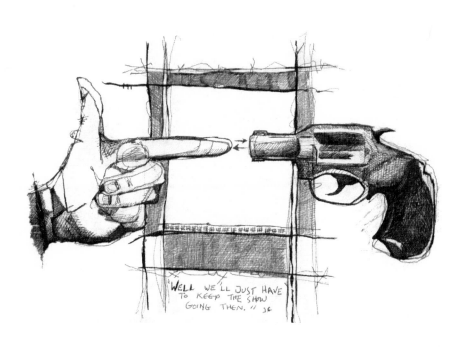

August 12, 1966–Present

I just said what I said
it was wrong
it was taken wrong
and now it is this.

Re: The Manuscript (be a friend and let me know if it sucks)

From: Everyman (friend@historyholdings.com)
Sent: Friday
To: Judas (traitormouth@hotmail.com)

You have to take out all of the Mother, Father, and Son—everything else reads as you—these poems read as you telling a story you heard. Example: if you want to talk about your Barbelo, talk about how she told you she was already dressing in black to mourn your soon-to-be Los Angeles freeway death—how you should be prepared to change your boyfriend's diapers because shit's all a twenty-year-older has to offer—all while at IHOP Easter breakfast, insisting that you steal a fork for her kitchen. That's your story—her addiction is her story and belongs to her.

My Musical-Faith in John Lennon Quakes with Recognition at Ronnie Hawkins's Power to Reconcile All

Ronnie admits, I didn't know
that much about the Beatles
at that time. My world
was brass knucks
and combat boots
everybody was still ruinin'
their livers. Ha ha aaa, ya
know there was no-
body in that love
peace thing in my crew.
Down there everybody
was still rockin' the lyrics—
      I'm gonna call up a gypsy woman on the telephone
      I'm gonna send out a worldwide hoo-doo—there
in China Ronnie is arrested
for carrying John's WAR IS OVER
IF YOU WANT IT—
Peace is easy, but hard to pay for—
Ronnie makes it out of Mao-ville
but John's Canadian Festival
for Peace is canceled.
John is shot gone,
      when Romping Ronnie survives
Cancer: You win some lose some,
I'm lucky to have made it this far
four lifetimes at least, maybe five.
While John waits for resurrection,
Ronnie Hawkins is asking
for VIAGRA® to go with his chemo.
Gotta treat all parts of a man—

Ronnie knows how to wait—
    forty days—
knows (in some form or another)
all things will come back home.
He swallows rum
and the devil shines down his throat.

There Is a Demon in You and I Want to See It

The mask turned out—re-ossifies—
skull retains origin shape, but red roots
       break to surface as blue—vines
growing up tresses. Fat in the sun—
       pools in limbs gone to rags.
Bones collect in the purse of intestines.
       Desire translated: possession—
an Apple bottom doll to sit on your face—
       and be eaten like nearly gone
rotten—juices rolling down your chin.
       Could you love this? This Angel
reversed—wrath inside-out—deviation?
       No? No. This is not what you
wanted—but asked for.

They Had Us Put Letters in My Grandmother's Coffin

At thirteen I wrote: *How could you leave me?*
In the corpse's hand, for 17 years this December,
a question unanswered—growing heavier as flesh
pulls back and bone goes to dust. The older I turn
the heavier the question—an understanding—how
selfish love—and no way to take back the letter.

Becoming Judas

1.

In loose robes of apple skins—
a sight path reaches towards
sternum as you collect silver.
Caiaphas' eyes run over your
adrenaline. You've got to get
out of there. You have a plan.
A way to keep the man-Jesus

    alive

        a little longer.

2.

You beg at his hem—bringing him
baskets of lavender & a blind girl
who births a child from her mouth
when describing color.

    *There is something worth
        keeping in this,*

3.

To Jesus who marks the end—
reconciling all to the One, you say,

    Will I know you in heaven?

Your heads touching as you lay in the grass
watching stars being devoured by clouds.
He laughs

What use is there in knowing me
if you are me, Judas?

4.

You hate this answer.

5.

I hate this answer.

6.

We simultaneously turn

7.

in our beds—away from salvation. Facing
white walls. Eventually I get up. Drink
coffee. Start writing again. Tattling again.

can you believe he was wearing that?
Red rope of apple peels.

8.

My poems are for those who'd rather eat
their ears than hear the sound of my voice.

Dear Other,
Do you know why I left?

I wasn't ready to be swallowed
by the fire of another.

9.

> *Don't go crazy on me now*
Jesus says as you choke—sobbing,
> *but I love you, I love. . .*

ripping wings off of bees to prepare
a gift—handfuls of weightless silver.

> *We can get out of here Jesus,*
> *you and me. Go someplace tropical.*

10.
I wipe steam off a mirror after a hot shower.
Face solemn from lack of sleep—a reflection
of Judas—dark opposite to the light we worship.
I refasten the silver-cord to my neck.
We ask,

> *How can I love you, the way that I do—*
> without having myself to loathe?

The Tree Judas Chose

was some ornamental thing—shape of a kidney—flowers veining over
its short and red-twisted trunk. Spent his
morning watching the long
tongued carpenter-bees
suckle its blossoms.

    As the Redbud wept its violet blooms, he caught the drops
    in his mouth—bruised their petals with his
    teeth, searching for that hushed
    light. Ate until his
    stomach ached

        from the bitter juices. Lips stained blue, he began to vomit
        a mellifluent river. The ground softened by his
        currents, turned to flesh. He built a body
        from this golden earth—a face
        that resembled Jesus.

    Before he could kiss the honey lips, a swarm of flies began
    to drink the shape away. Their wings shining
    like silver coins tossed into the air. He
    devoured them in an attempt
    to taste sweetness.

When he jumped, his soul broke into a thousand pieces—an army
of snakeflies humming—a chorus of apologies dying
in small increments—like a lesson in letting go
learned one fall at a time.

Resolves and Reversals:
You Say Goodbye and I Say Hello

Flip of a Coin

Maybe today all pennies
will come up heads for Judas
and give misery a rest.
Bad news for us though,
with our lotto tickets worn
to the softness of skin
from the constant touch
of our wishing hands.

Change These Bones

> . . . each pleasure and pain is a sort of nail which nails and rivets the soul
> to the body, and engrosses her and makes her believe . . .
>
> —Socrates

I haven't seen my mother in months. She sleeps with the television on. Her mouth shines and dims with the plot shifts of late night commercials. The blue hue flattens her to the depth of bed sheets. Her gums are bleached by pus pressing against containment. I lay myself next to her under covers of cigarette smoke; I find the hidden scent of effort in washed linens. She's trying to keep clean.

She refuses to see a doctor. She says, *you wouldn't pity me if you knew how intensely I dream.* She says, *life is short, but it is also long, so goddamn long.* Her molars are cracked like ice in coffee. At breakfast I'll ask her to see a dentist. We know he'll tell her they all have to go. Wrench each little white horse from its hill by breaking them off at the knees. He will take all the bad bones out from her. He will make her whole again.

Instructions to Understanding Mother

Unhitch her. Take her apart one layer at a time. Gut her. Don't stop, not even at the recognition of origins—warm as a newborn in your hands.

———————

Taking yourself off will be more difficult. Hook your thumbs under your eyelids. Pull until the skin snaps off like a latex glove. Unravel the red twine of flesh and knit it into a scarf. Snap your bones into a pile of twigs to nest your egg-frail eyes. Wad the pumps and valves into a laundry basket. Take what's left and proceed to the next step.

———————

Link her bones with rubber bands. Blow the heart up and stick it to the ribs with pink chewing gum. Plop the brain into the skull like hot oatmeal in a bowl. Install the muscle and gristle, same as you would a chicken wire fence. Wrap the skin like a quilt around the corpse. Insert yourself through the coin-slot mouth. Now, you are her.

———————

I'd call you, but you only hear a drug addict. I've all but disappeared. But in me is a world of inexpressible light. What if I told you—

I have felt the hand of the sun, with its thousand fingers sprouting new hands at every touch—I have cried a spider-infested ivy that chokes me in my sleep—I have missed you until a knot of roots has claimed all the earth of me—Remember, you and I were once the same fistful of dirt. Come home.

The Lady of Babylon
at the Moment of Judgment

—The Seven Angels Show—

To replace the need for memory
she collects in a metal cup
the color of sex spittle and blood

She sits upon a silver blanket
knitted from spun tears. Her skin
is draped with gold strung pearls.

Ask her to love you and she will
pluck one shinning sore to place
on your tongue. Nacre will out-

grow your words. The mantle
of your sorrows softening the jewel
to a fish-eye—with this new vision

guarding against approach—mascara
running down her checks, she pounds
on the chest of heaven, screaming,

I am not a widow, and I will never mourn.

—The Seven Angels Warn—

Come out of her body
like a tent whose ceiling is held
up by the breath of multitudes—
sighs of want and frustration.

Acquisition is loss in disguise.
Take off the purple velvet robe.
Be naked as the day the armor
of your mother came off.

Hear the wind—
constant whisper on your skin
reminding you, We are all so fragile. Be kind.

—The Lord God Who Judges Her—

has her drink from her own cup. The writing on her forehead falls to the ground. She reads, *I was someone's mother.* A fire swells in her bones. She mourns and a thousand sparks leap from her throat to devour the city in light.

In the Hour of Temptation,
I Get My Punk Rock Self Back

The fist-sized hailstones stop
     falling. Hillside fires hiss
to silence. I do the splits. In the grass,
     fresh green tongues lick my thighs.
Love collects in my purse, like silver
     rain. Rummaged from the bottom
of my bag, I pull the tear shaped coins
     to pay for flesh to dress up the dead.
We play cops and robbers. I'm the robber.
     I scold my son for becoming
older. He shrinks back into
     the knot of my center—
like all loss—forgotten.
     I rub handfuls of earth
over my skin. The rocks are a million
     gestures of kindness—detached
fingers strumming a heavy base line
     over the sound of my second name.

Mother,

When I thought the light had left me
it was you who made me swallow
that chain of mirrors to catch the vision
of fire rippling across bramble—waves
of heat moving like silk where I snapped
my bones for kindling. It was you who
clawed out from that layered husk
of gossamer to put my collar bone back
on—showed me I was more than broken—
taught me, we are more than our mistakes.
You made me—unmade me. And from
the raveling and unraveling you gave me
a tapestry—image of women passing
the small stone of memory—hand to hand—
bridging generations. You who stands despite
their arm-sized cords: you who understands life
is granted daily. Through you I am born
again, again, again. In a gathering of light.

December 1980

The Gospel of Judas is stolen from a male antiquities dealer.
The heist is organized by a woman with well-manicured nails.
She runs her reds under the purple lining of his jacket. He lets her
take photos of his entire collection. He poses next to the door lock.

———————

Judas sold Jesus for thirty silver pieces and / or a kiss. As a traitor,
my bets are on the long shot kiss. It's my only chance at winning.

———————

Mark D. Chapman has just finished catching small children
from jumping off of cliffs when he decides to take a trip to New
York. He is tired of everyone looking towards the wrong light.
John Lennon is no Jesus. No sir. The phonies got to go. Yes sir.

———————

I break into this world while my mother is working at an antique shop.
I christen a Victorian rug with embryonic fluid. The old is stained new.

———————

No one yet has read the codex. No one knows it's Judas howling in
that papyrus. The antiquities dealer gets the scrolls back. The woman
disappears. What are the chances that gun shots are synchronized—
bullets organized into choirs to make harmonies of this world—

———————

I want to believe we're mimics of the divine. John Lennon accepts
Chapman's kiss with gratitude. All is done in, with, and for Love.

———————

Judas is locked in a safety deposit box in Hicksville, New York; rotten humidity eating chunks out of his words. A gun is grown into the flesh of Chapman's hand. John Lennon bleeds on the steps of the Dakota. I recognizing color for the first time. My eyes focused on mother's light.

―――――――――

Jesus says, *forgive you, if you forgive me.* Judas says, *forgiven you, but I won't forgive me.* Jesus says, *well, we'll just have to keep this show going then.*

―――――――――

Mother says, *I didn't mean to burn you.* I am too young to understand— language: fire is a verb substitution for love.

Biographical Note: Cheryl Gross

Born and raised in Brooklyn, Cheryl Gross started her career as an illustrator and painter. Her work has graced the walls of galleries and museums throughout the world, including Laforet Museum in Japan, The Brooklyn Museum, and The Museum of the City of New York. Cheryl is an Adjunct Professor in the Communications Department at Pratt Institute, where she teaches illustration and motion graphics. She is also a Visiting Instructor at Bloomfield College in New Jersey.

Biographical Note: Nicelle Davis

Originally from Utah, Nicelle Davis now resides in Lancaster, California, with her son, J.J. *Becoming Judas* is her second book. Her first book, *Circe*, is available from Lowbrow Press. Her third collection, *In the Circus of You*, will be released by Rose Metal Press in 2014. Her poems have appeared or are forthcoming in *The Beloit Poetry Journal*, *The New York Quarterly*, *PANK*, *SLAB Magazine*, *Two Review*, and others. You can read her e-chapbooks at Gold Wake Press and Whale Sound. She is the director of the Living Poetry Project. She runs a free online poetry workshop at The Bees' Knees Blog, is an assistant poetry editor for *Connotation Press* and is the assistant managing editor for the *Los Angeles Review*. She has taught poetry at Youth for Positive Change, an organization that promotes success for youth in secondary schools, and with Volunteers of America in their Homeless Youth Center. She currently teaches at Antelope Valley College.

Thank you:
My Families.